The Coming of the Kings

THE COMING
OF THE KINGS

and Other Plays

TED HUGHES

FABER & FABER
London · Boston

First published in 1970
by Faber and Faber Limited
3 Queen Square London WC1
Reprinted 1972, 1976 and 1979
Printed in Great Britain by
Whitstable Litho Ltd., Whitstable, Kent
All rights reserved

ISBN 0 571 09562 3

All applications for professional and amateur rights in these plays should be addressed to Miss Olwyn Hughes, Flat B, 10 Arkwright Road, London, NW3.

Contents

Author's Note

These plays were originally
written for broadcasting and full
stage directions are not provided
except in *The Coming of the Kings*.
However, all the plays can very
easily be adapted for stage
performance.

The Coming of the Kings

Characters

THE FORTUNE-TELLER
THE INNKEEPER
HIS WIFE
THE PRIEST
THE BUSINESSMAN
THE POLICE INSPECTOR
THE MINSTREL
JOSEPH
MARY
THE THREE KINGS

The Coming of the Kings

*The road leads in from the right-back, towards the audience,
dividing the Inn, on the left, from the tumbledown animal shed on
the right. The Inn is red, with white door and window frames.
Out over the door hangs a large sign:* THE EMPEROR'S HEAD,
*from which dangles a giant reproduction of a Roman Coin, with a
head crudely painted on it. The cottage is black, with loose
sacking over the windows and the door which, lifted aside, would
reveal most of the interior.*

A cock crows.
The FORTUNE-TELLER *appears, trudging down the road
towards the audience. He stops, yawns, shifts his pack. At that
moment, a deafening commotion from the shed on the right:
kicking sounds, violent bangs, and the prolonged lusty braying
of a donkey.* FORTUNE-TELLER *drops his pack in surprise,
stares at the shed in amazement. Bedroom window of the inn
slams open, innkeeper's* WIFE's *head appears: she yells at the
top of her voice.*

WIFE: All night long you've been at it!
When will you shut up your racket!
Shut up, you ugly brute, you!
Or I'll get my husband to shoot you.
*The donkey is silenced. Her head disappears and the window
whams shut. The* FORTUNE-TELLER *looks to and fro between the*

shed and the inn.
He tiptoes towards the shed, listens.
An ox lows.
The FORTUNE-TELLER *starts, listens again.*

FORTUNE-TELLER: What's that? What did you say?
[*Ox lows.*]
What? Here? Today?
[*Ox lows.*]
That's what I thought you said.
[*Ox lows.*]
Oh, my poor head!
But that's incredible!
[*Cock crows.*]
What's that? You say it's true?
[*Dog barks.*]
You too? You too?
Oh, now what shall I do!
Donkey begins to bray and kick up a tremendous din.
Inn door opens, and out comes the INNKEEPER *in his nightcap*
and nightshirt, waving a thick stick. Bedroom window opens
and his WIFE's *head sticks out.*

WIFE: Batter the brute with your stick
Till where he's thin he goes thick
And where he's thick he goes thin.
Silence the monster's din.
I haven't had a wink all night . . .
No wonder I look such a sight.

FORTUNE-TELLER: Stop! What will you do?

INNKEEPER: I'll hammer the donkey black and blue
And the ox I'll hammer pink.
All night we've not had a wink
For their mooing and creaking and braying . . .

FORTUNE-TELLER: But don't you hear what they're saying?

INNKEEPER: Saying? Are you right in the head?

FORTUNE-TELLER: Didn't you hear what the donkey said?

INNKEEPER: Now you're a peculiar feller!

WIFE: Is that that fortune-teller?

FORTUNE-TELLER: Madame, at your service. If you've a
wrinkle in your palm, I'll read it: there's health, wealth
and beauty in wrinkles, if you get the right man to read
them. The more wrinkles you have, the more there is to
read for your fortune, so the more fortune for you.
That's a lucky face, lady.

WIFE: I've heard of you. Wait. I'll be down.
Her head disappears.

INNKEEPER: Have you just arrived in town?

FORTUNE-TELLER: I know where the money lies.

INNKEEPER: Well, this town has plenty of flies.
But money? Think again.
I have to scrape like a hen.
I've had to sell my brother for a slave.
It's so difficult here to save.
Enter WIFE *from inn.*

WIFE: Fortune-teller!

FORTUNE-TELLER: Madame!

WIFE: Oh, please read my palm.
What does it say, quick? Oh, I feel funny.

FORTUNE-TELLER: First, you cross my palm with money.

WIFE: How much?

FORTUNE-TELLER: Let it be silver.

INNKEEPER: *Stop!*
WIFE *turns on her husband furiously, while* FORTUNE-TELLER
holds and inspects her palm.

WIFE: Have you mended my wobbly mop?
Have you nailed the carpet down?
Or flattened the nail that catches in my gown?
Or oiled the door and the kitchen pump?
What are you standing there for, you lump?

13

INNKEEPER: Week in week out, and never a guest,
    And you give silver to this pest?
WIFE: Then why did you want to keep an inn?
    Think of the lady I might have been
    If you'd had guts enough to launch
    That pudding barrel elephant paunch
    Into some trade with better . . .
FORTUNE-TELLER: Money!
WIFE: What?
INNKEEPER: What's that?
FORTUNE-TELLER: I read here
    That the greatest good luck in a million year
    Is coming your way.
INNKEEPER: What? Where? *When?*
FORTUNE-TELLER [*still studying the* WIFE's *palm*]: Today.
WIFE: Today?
FORTUNE-TELLER: The King Of Men
    Is going to visit your inn—today.
INNKEEPER: What? What's that? What do you say?
FORTUNE-TELLER: Be prepared.
INNKEEPER: A king?
FORTUNE-TELLER: Three *kings*.
INNKEEPER: Beyond my wildest imaginings!
    To stay with us here?
FORTUNE-TELLER: To visit this inn.
    A new age is going to begin
    From what occurs at this inn today.
    And you will be famous for ever.
WIFE: For ever!
INNKEEPER: Now who's stupid? Now who's clever?
    I bought this inn ten years ago
    For this moment. What else do you know?
FORTUNE-TELLER: Prepare.
WIFE: Three Kings!

14

INNKEEPER: When we've had them,
Every night after, we'll be crammed full.
We'll be on the map, the fashionable
Most famous Inn in Bethlehem.
We'll make a fortune!

WIFE [*in great excitement*]: Get the place clean.
Some of those rooms aren't fit to be seen.
Scrub them, sweep them, quick, quick, quick, and
Get the flea-powder.

INNKEEPER: Get the chickens
Out of the bath.

WIFE: Get all the dogs
And their pups out of the beds and the hogs
And the hoglets out of the cupboards and scatter
Disinfectant. What's the matter?

INNKEEPER [*he is standing almost in a trance*]: This is the greatest
day of my life!

WIFE: And as usual you've to thank your wife.
Get a move on.
They dash into the inn. Through what follows the WIFE *is
throwing bundles of rags, broken chairs, picture frames, etc. out
of the windows. Soon the* INNKEEPER *re-emerges dressed and
begins to carry the junk into the shed. But first:*

FORTUNE-TELLER: I told them no more than the true.
But I have not told it all.
A cloud wrote on the blue
That a world is about to fall
Out of mind and care;
Along with the rest, these two:
This penny-shoveller,
His ghost shall be trapped in the bell
Of a Grocer's till, and shall cry
Every sale with a yell
Of envious agony:

15

Throughout eternity
That shall be his Hell.
And his grasping wife
Who would have beaten the ass,
She shall stare eternity out
Trapped in a looking-glass.
Exit the FORTUNE-TELLER.
Enter the INNKEEPER, *loads himself with flotsam.*

INNKEEPER: The lazy dog will miss his chance,
But the ambitious dog will dance
And so will I. When luck arrives
It's the ready man who thrives.
Others awake when it's flown past . . .
But I'm the ready man at last.
I shall not miss it, I shall not miss it!
I'll catch it by the wings and kiss it.
WIFE *throws down a basketwork cradle from the bedroom, it hits him.*

WIFE: Dump this old cradle into the shed.
Have you fixed the attic bed?
[*She continues until he has flung all the rubbish into the shed and scurried back into the inn.*]
Have you polished the brass door-knobs?
There are about a thousand jobs.
Have you scrubbed the table-top?
A new hinge on the cellar-drop?
Have you brought the barrels up?
Hurry up! Hurry up! Hurry up! Hurry up!

INNKEEPER: Yes, yes, yes . . .
[*He is about to re-enter the inn when he stops, stares. A priest in sumptuous robes enters.*]
Er—your majes—er, your Lordship—er, your honour . . .

PRIEST: Your Grace.

INNKEEPER: Your Grace?

16

PRIEST: As you see, I'm a high priest of the temple.

My means and my spirituality are equally ample.

That is to say . . . I'm a power on earth, and in heaven.

That is to say . . . do you follow me? Yes?

INNKEEPER: Your Grace.

He bows, he kneels, he bumps his forehead on the ground.

PRIEST [*pompous*]: No need to bang your head so hard on the street.

It's quite enough if you kneel. Both knees. I repeat:

When you look at me, do you feel yourself quake?

That's the devil in you. I'm more than he can take.

You know the most evil things in this world, what they are?

They are troublesome new religious ideas. Heavens! I could swear,

I could curse the ears off an elephant,

When I think of the wickedness of people!

[*He grows enraged.*]

I will not permit them to think whatever they want,

I want their souls, I tell you, tethered to my steeple.

I want them in my fold. In my power.

I will not let them out of my grasp. I want to see them cower

Under the purity of my glare

When I see them sitting so wicked there!

Oh!

INNKEEPER: Yes, your Grace.

PRIEST: And now do you know what's come to my ear?

An illegal religious festival is going to be held. Here.

Well?

INNKEEPER: Your Grace, I——

PRIEST: The wickedness! The wickedness!

People think they can have heavenly happiness

Without my permission. They want to be able to pray

Without paying me money! Though my money's all
taken away

By Great Herod to pay for his army.

INNKEEPER: Your Grace——

PRIEST: Where are the vandals? Don't deny it to my face.

INNKEEPER: Your Grace—I don't know what you're talking
about.

PRIEST: You say so. Very well. I shall stay. I shall sit them
out.

I'll stay here in your inn till I hear their revels,

Then I'll descend in the Hand of God and cast out their
devils

And deliver them over to Herod who knows full well

That these new religions come from Hell.

Lead me to a room.

INNKEEPER [*scrambling up*]: Your Grace.

PRIEST: And bring me wine.

And bring me roasted quails. I might as well dine.

PRIEST *follows the* INNKEEPER *into the inn.*

Enter, in a bowler, and humming "Three Blind Mice", a
BUSINESSMAN. *He studies the inn.*

Re-enter INNKEEPER *and* WIFE, *in great excitement.*

WIFE: What's he talking about?

INNKEEPER: I don't *know.*

WIFE: Illegal religious festival?

INNKEEPER: He says *so.*

WIFE: But whatever can he mean?

INNKEEPER: That's it. What can he mean?

WIFE: And is he paying for the wine?

INNKEEPER: We'll send him the bill.

WIFE: But he's a great man. He'll advertise us, he will.

I mean, just by being here. Get him his quails.

INNKEEPER: I've sent. We must put on a great banquet, for
if today's fails——

WIFE: Don't you see? It's beginning. Our luck's begun.

INNKEEPER: O let me be wealthy for ever before today's done.

WIFE: Get about it, you idiot.

She goes, he stands, calculating on his fingers the items he needs to remember, flustered and pressed.

BUSINESSMAN: So this is "The Emperor's Head". Then this is
the one.

INNKEEPER [*startled*]: Your Grace?

BUSINESSMAN: What?

INNKEEPER: I mean, sir, is there——

BUSINESSMAN: Tell me, my good man,
I've heard there's going to be a world-famous magician
Performing an earth-shaking exhibition
Of miracles here today. Have you heard?

INNKEEPER: Magician? Here? Today? Not a word.

BUSINESSMAN: One of those Holy Men who walk on fire,
Tie venomous snakes in knots without any fear,
Turn a sardine into a cartload of cod,
Bring the rain down like Almighty God,
Convert a crust of bread into a whole field of barley—
One of those Holy wonders. Maybe I'm a bit early——

INNKEEPER: I've heard nothing about it, sir.

BUSINESSMAN: Come, come,
Some rival interest's paid you to keep mum.
Eh?

INNKEEPER: Rival interest?

BUSINESSMAN: Well, well, well.
Don't think I'm going to be fooled. It's valuable—
A show like this. I sign him on, see?
Wait a minute, maybe you don't know me.

INNKEEPER: I'm afraid, sir, er, I . . .

BUSINESSMAN: Socrates D. Conkhorse.
I'll sell anything—reasonable of course.
I don't try to sell the moon, though some would buy.

You must understand, I'm a plain honest guy.
I sell untried gladiators by tens,
Rope-sandals by millions, dwarfs with wens
By the brace. Would you like a crocodile?
Or a beautiful slave-girl plus the coconut isle?
Cash down and it's yours.

INNKEEPER: As a matter of fact, my sandals are a bit
    frayed——

BUSINESSMAN: And with this miracle-worker, I'm made!
A man who can raise the dead! That's really new!
I sign him on at forty per cent and—Phew!
It makes me sweat to think of the fortune going.
Look, five per cent for you, just for showing
Where he's lodging.

INNKEEPER: But I don't quite see——

BUSINESSMAN: Look: ten pounds, and he'll raise your aunt or
    your uncle. Agree?
A hundred pounds to raise a grandad. Three
Thousand to raise a father. There's no limit!
Don't you want to make a fortune, dammit?
Where is he? O.K. You're going to play dumb?
Well, I'll stay here in this hotel till he's come.
I'll hear him by his crowd.

INNKEEPER: You can stay gladly.

BUSINESSMAN: But understand, I think you've served me badly.
Bring me some beer in, and I'd like some beef.

INNKEEPER: Straight ahead, sir.

As the INNKEEPER *and the* BUSINESSMAN *enter the inn a*
POLICE INSPECTOR *saunters in, stops, surveys the shed and the*
inn, consulting his notebook. Re-enter the INNKEEPER *and his*
WIFE *talking together excitedly.*

WIFE: It's beyond belief.

INNKEEPER: We've never had such guests in our lives.

WIFE: Fortune comes to the one who believes

All that the fortune-teller says.

INNKEEPER: I'll have to run down into the town.
We need more food. Oh, day of days!

WIFE: Hurry up and get it, you clown!

WIFE *re-enters the inn, the* INNKEEPER *is about to dash off when he sees the* POLICE INSPECTOR.

POLICE INSPECTOR: The Emperor's Head. Hm!
[*Consulting his book.*]
Opposite, a shed
Of god-forsaken ruinous aspect. The shed!
This must be the place. Hm!
[*Shuts his book.*]
And you're the proprietor?

INNKEEPER: That's right, Inspector. Anything wrong?

POLICE INSPECTOR: We haven't met before?

INNKEEPER: No.

POLICE INSPECTOR: Sure?

INNKEEPER: Yes.

POLICE INSPECTOR: What are your politics?

INNKEEPER: I haven't any.

POLICE INSPECTOR: Be careful.

INNKEEPER: I agree with all tax.

POLICE INSPECTOR: Good for you. Well, well, and who'd have
thought!

INNKEEPER: What's wrong, Inspector?

POLICE INSPECTOR: Who's staying with you? Straight out,
Don't stop to invent a lie.

INNKEEPER: Guests?

POLICE INSPECTOR: Who?

INNKEEPER: A high priest of the Temple. And a businessman.
Just two.

POLICE INSPECTOR: And what do you know about this demon-
stration?
Don't put on that dumbfounded, ox-like expression.

21

It's been brought to our notice that today
A Political Agitator is going to say his say
Here at "The Emperor's Head", and threaten our state
With red-hot ideas, turbulence of passion
To shake our law and order out of fashion,
Make people discontented with their noses,
And shoot at policemen, and trample the palace roses
With peering in at the windows carrying knives.
Herod's court are in terror of their lives.
What have you to say?

INNKEEPER: Me? I'm just an innkeeper.

POLICE INSPECTOR: Politically, you're a dangerous sleeper.
It's men like you who let the matches catch,
Who let the fireflies of rebellion hatch.

INNKEEPER: I don't know what you're talking about.

POLICE INSPECTOR: Well then,
Where is the crowd assembled to hear this man?

INNKEEPER: Which man?

POLICE INSPECTOR: This revolutionary with his message for
the people which
Is going to shake Herod and cause a hitch
In the smooth running of great Caesar's lands?
I've got to catch him. Stop wringing your hands.

INNKEEPER: I just don't know what all this is about.

POLICE INSPECTOR: Haven't you seen some bearded ferocious
figure
With a dagger like a bread-knife only bigger,
Whispering to a dozen like himself?
He wants to topple Herod off the shelf.
I can't decide whether you're innocent
Or only bluffing.

INNKEEPER: Please, Inspector, don't.
I don't know what's come over me today.
I hardly understand what people say.

POLICE INSPECTOR: All right then. I'll stay here, in your
    pleasant inn.
    And when this fellow's followers begin
    To gather to hear him speak—I shall be peeping.
    Today, the State's safety is in my keeping.
    Show me a room.
INNKEEPER: Certainly, Inspector.
POLICE INSPECTOR: If this man's the disease, then I'm the
    doctor.
    Bring me a barrel of wine and a boar's head.
    I'll fix a hundred of them when I've fed.
    Exit the INNKEEPER *with the* POLICE INSPECTOR.
    Enter the wandering MINSTREL, *in beggarly raiment. He stands
    looking at the shed. He lifts the sacking and peers in.*
    Re-enter INNKEEPER *and his* WIFE, *excited as before.*
INNKEEPER: It's beyond me.
WIFE: Three of them!
INNKEEPER: The Great of Jerusalem!
WIFE: But *three*.
INNKEEPER: Yes, and the greatest!
WIFE: *Three*.
INNKEEPER: This Inspector, the latest,
    He fairly made me sweat!
    Now they're downing all they can get.
    The High Priest's drunk a crate.
    He's joined with the businessman.
    But what do they all mean?
    What are they waiting for?
    One man, or three, or more?
    An illegal religious meeting?
    A fire-walking, fire-eating
    Magician, or a revolt?
    I'm sure it's not my fault.
WIFE: I've got it!

INNKEEPER: What?

WIFE: Three!

INNKEEPER: What do you mean? I don't see.

WIFE: The three kings are these three.
The Fortune-teller told
There would be Three, and—behold.

INNKEEPER: These three are Kings?

WIFE: Aren't they?

INNKEEPER: Disguised, do you mean to say?

WIFE [*dancing*]: Kings! Kings!
What wonderful creatures are Kings!

INNKEEPER [*still incredulous*]: And we've got a houseful?

WIFE: Isn't it blissful?

INNKEEPER [*suddenly going wild*]: We shall make a fortune!
We're made!
They'll say: "That's where *They* stayed."

BOTH: Kings! Kings! O Wonderful things. . . .

They dance around together, but break apart seeing the
MINSTREL.

INNKEEPER: Who's that? What's he doing peering into my old
stable?

The MINSTREL *comes forward, as if not seeing the two.*

MINSTREL: The hills were against me.
The sharp, peevish edges of the road-stones were against
me,
And the thorns were against me,
But I made my way.

The dogs were with me, one brought me a ham-bone.
The birds were with me and showed me fresh eggs,
And the stream, the stream
Came out of its way to clear itself at my feet.

By these signs a traveller knows

The moving spirits are friendly.

And here is the place: The Emperor's Head.

The Emperor's head that spoke to me in a dream——

INNKEEPER: Hey, you, rags, what do you want?

MINSTREL: Food and a bed.

I have come a long way with a fever in my head.

INNKEEPER: Do you know where you are?

MINSTREL: I am under the sun, the god-given day-star.

INNKEEPER: Don't you know where you're standing?

MINSTREL: On an earth of the Creator's making and lending.

INNKEEPER: Do you know who you're speaking to?

WIFE: Yes, just whose pig-keeper are you?

Your toes are insulting the sky.

The birds have slept in your hair.

Your trousers are ready to die,

Your coat's only just there.

You're like a rat's nest walking.

Are you begging or hawking?

MINSTREL: Any bed and a slice of bread

To keep the soul in my body, lady.

WIFE: Away with you, you rubbish heap.

This is an Inn where Great Kings sleep.

He's one of those disreputable minstrels.

Upper window opens, PRIEST's *head appears.*

PRIEST: More wine up here! Service! Do you hear?

BUSINESSMAN's *head appears.*

BUSINESSMAN: Get more beef up and more beer.

WIFE: Coming, sir.

She runs into the inn.

INNKEEPER: Well, you heard that.

Now what are you staring at?

MINSTREL: Look at that star.

INNKEEPER: It's only a star.

MINSTREL: But it's shining by day.

Upper window opens again and the WIFE's *angry head sticks out.*

WIFE: There you still are!

Hurry up, man. More food and more drink.

Don't stand gaping like the kitchen sink.

The head vanishes and the window bangs.

INNKEEPER: You'd better be off. And I'd better hurry.

As you see, we're full up. I'm sorry.

INNKEEPER *runs off.* MINSTREL *stands as he was.*

MINSTREL: What a King of Men is Greedy!

Penny calls to penny, stronger than a man.

Floors call to carpets, stronger than a man.

Tables call to linen, stronger than a man.

Walls call to paintings, stronger than a man.

For a man's mind is money's slave.

The poor torn coat calls to the silk lining,

The old split bowl to figured silver,

The dirty dry glass to the vineyards

The rough bread calls to the sturgeon—

And a man goes running their errands

For a man's mind is money's slave.

Bow down, bow down and worship

The big belly of the cash-bank

That has swallowed so many slaves.

May you all go to the heaven

Of a crumbling junk-heap.

[*During this the stage has darkened: he turns to the shed.*]

Now night falls on the mountain valleys and in the
    gardens.

Now the cold comes down

Murdering the small birds in their feathers as they sleep.

The fish in ponds lose consciousness with the cold.

I'll creep in here and the breath of an ox and a donkey

26

Will do me for blankets. These are hard times
For those who cannot persuade themselves to rob.
He goes into the shed.
The three guests are singing "Three Blind Mice" as a round-song.

JOSEPH *and* MARY *come up the road and stop in front of the inn.*
JOSEPH: We have come a long way. We can't go farther
tonight, in the cold. The snow is beginning to prickle
our faces. If this inn's full up, the Lord knows what we
shall do. I'll knock.
JOSEPH *knocks. The* INNKEEPER *comes scampering up, returning
from his errand of ordering more food. He doesn't notice that*
JOSEPH *has knocked.*
INNKEEPER: Brrr! What a night! Hello—is your wife ill? She
looks as if she might need a doctor. You ought to look
after her, old man.
[*He speaks to audience.*]
These people who wander about the roads are terrible.
They treat each other like rats and mice: no feelings at
all. Brr!
He goes in, shuts the door.
JOSEPH: I'll try again.
[*He knocks.* WIFE *looks out.*]
We need a room. And my wife here needs a bed.
WIFE: Sorry, full up.
She bangs the door to.
JOSEPH: Now what shall we do?
Door opens, the INNKEEPER *comes out.*
INNKEEPER: I'm terribly sorry. I think I ought to explain.
You see that sign: it says "The Emperor's Head".
That is to say, it's a hostel for Emperors—Kings.
Kings as Kings, or incognito Kings.
Those three fine voices come from the throats of Kings
Who may well be pretending not to be Kings.

And I'm reserving three rooms for three Kings
Who whether they come disguised or else as Kings
Will still demand I treat them all as Kings.
And can a man of my sort deny Kings?
Kings made me, and Kings keep me. I am the King's.
You understand? You can sleep in that shed.
You do understand that I can't do differently?
He runs back into the hotel.

JOSEPH: We're out of luck. Go in.
They go into the shed. "Three Blind Mice" rises and falls away.
"We Three Kings" heard faintly in the distance.
"Three Blind Mice" rises again, falls away behind what
follows.
Enter INNKEEPER *and his* WIFE *arguing.*

INNKEEPER: But if these are Kings we could be renting
The three empty rooms. Two here were wanting
A room just now. And they'd have paid.

WIFE: And if they're not Kings, but just what they said?
Then the three Kings will be coming tonight.
The Fortune-teller's proving right
In everything else, so why not in this?
We can't afford to miss what we'd miss.
Those three rooms must be kept for the Kings
Who will be coming if these are not Kings.
I'm freezing. Anyway you're wrong. These *are* the Kings.

INNKEEPER: They don't behave much like Kings.

WIFE: Do you mean because they're blotto?
"The customer's always right" is my motto.
Bring up more wine, in case more Kings come.
You are so unbelievably dumb.
She goes in, INNKEEPER *runs in after.*

INNKEEPER: I'm only afraid I'm losing money!
"We Three Kings" is now quite loud.
MINSTREL *comes staggering out of the shed, shaking his head,*

rousing himself. He stands, collecting his wits. Something amazing has happened to him.

MINSTREL: I've just had an astounding dream as I lay in the
straw.
I dreamed a star fell on to the straw beside me
And lay blazing. Then when I looked up
I saw a bull come flying through a sky of fire
And on its shoulders a huge silver woman
Holding the moon. And afterwards there came
A donkey flying through that same burning heaven
And on its shoulders a colossal man
Holding the sun. Suddenly I awoke
And saw a bull and a donkey kneeling in the straw,
And the great moving shadows of a man and a woman—
I say they were a man and a woman but
I dare not say what I think they were. I did not dare to
look.
I ran out here into the freezing world
Because I dared not look. Inside that shed.
As he turns to look at the shed, he sees something down the road where before he had seen the star by day. The INNKEEPER *comes out of the inn, pausing in the open doorway.*

INNKEEPER: What do you say?
WIFE: I said get more logs.
INNKEEPER: I heard. I have only a man's legs.
I don't have a stag's or a running dog's.
[*Now to the* MINSTREL.]
What's the matter with you?
You look so white you look blue.
What are you staring at?
MINSTREL: Look.
INNKEEPER *follows the direction of* MINSTREL'*s finger, stares, then drops the log basket he is carrying and bolts into the inn.*
INNKEEPER: Wife! Wife! Quick! Look at this!

MINSTREL: A star is coming this way along the road.
    If I were not standing upright, this would be a dream.
    A star the shape of a sword of fire, point-downward,
    Is floating along the road. And now it rises.
    It is shaking fire on to the roofs and the gardens.
    [*Star appears, suspended, rising slowly from behind till it comes to rest directly over the animal shed.*]
    And now it rises above the animal shed
    Where I slept till the dream woke me. And now
    The star is standing over the animal shed.
    During this speech, as the star rose to its position, a light kindled within the shed, and now light is beaming from every crevice.
    "We Three Kings" at full volume, so much as may not drown the speech.
    Re-enter, from the inn, INNKEEPER *and* WIFE. *He points not at the star but down the road up which it has come.*

INNKEEPER: Look, if those are not three Kings, I'm a turnip.

WIFE: Oh, bless that Fortune-teller. It's the Kings.
    Enter, majestically, fully arrayed, the three KINGS.
    INNKEEPER *and his* WIFE *fall on their knees.*

INNKEEPER: This way, your Majesties.
    Everything's prepared for your ease.
    A banquet to tickle your eyes.

WIFE: We're roasting a dozen sucking pigs.

INNKEEPER: We're basting them with brandied figs.

WIFE: We've hired a little orchestra
    To help you down the vintage-jar.

INNKEEPER: Our motto is "Guests, stuff your gullets
    Till your buttons fly like bullets"—
    Er—your Majesties—this—this
    This is the inn. Your Majesties!
    That's only a horrible old place where I keep my donkey and my old bull and my rubbish—your Majesties!

The three KINGS *ignore the inn and the* INNKEEPER, *their attention is on the stable.*

FIRST KING: We have followed the star over mountains
Where the stones cried and the thorns were broken.
We have followed the star over deserts
Where the rocks split at the touch of the night cold,
We have followed the beckoning of that star
Till it stands where it stands. We have arrived.

SECOND KING: He will be born to the coughing of animals
Among the broken, rejected objects
In the corner that costs not a penny
In the darkness of the mouse and the spider.

The THIRD KING *has lifted aside the sacking front of the shed.*

THIRD KING: He is here. The King of the Three Worlds
Has been born and is here.

The three KINGS *enter the shed, leaving the sacking wide, the light blazing out from the interior.*

Snow has started to fall and is now coming down in thick windless flakes.

"Once in Royal David's City" begins softly, taking over from "We Three Kings" which faded as they spoke.

INNKEEPER *and his* WIFE *are still kneeling.*

INNKEEPER: What? What are they saying? Where are they
going? Who's been born? What's happening?
Why are the three great kings going into my old stable?
Why is that star standing over the roof of my old stable?
Who has lit that great light inside my old stable?
What is happening? Why doesn't somebody tell me? What's
going on in my old stable?

"Once in Royal David's City" now loud. MINSTREL *stands in stage-centre, under the thickly falling snow.*

MINSTREL: Listen. The snow is falling.
Snow is falling on all the roads.
Falling on to the hills, on to the eyelashes of sheep.

31

Falling into the chimneys and on to the doorsteps,
Into the frozen well, into the dark forest.
Slowly the heavens are falling.
Every snowflake is an angel.
The angels are settling on the world.
The world will be white with angels.
The world will be deep in angels.

"Once in Royal David's City" now very loud. The MINSTREL
stands in the large falling flakes. The INNKEEPER *and his* WIFE,
*as they were, bewildered and overawed, kneel in the snow. The
manger scene is silhouetted in the great golden light beaming
from the stable under the large bright star.*

The Tiger's Bones

Characters

THE GUARDIAN SPIRIT

DULLY

JITTERWIT

VON GONKTOP

THE MASTER

CHIEF UGGLAMUGGLA

SAVAGES

THE OVERSEER

THE SAGE

The Tiger's Bones

Enter GUARDIAN SPIRIT.

GUARDIAN SPIRIT: I am a guardian spirit.
Never mind whose.
I am here to show you a strange happening.
Whether you believe it or not
Does not matter
Because it is quite true, and doesn't need your belief
To help it.
Here is a scene with trees, an inn, and a road.
Dawn is just opening.
A man comes round the side of the inn
And sits on a bench, under the window.
He is carrying heavy bags.
He has been sleeping in an outhouse.
He cannot see me, for he is a human being.
He speaks.
DULLY *has entered, carrying two big kitbags. He sits, yawns,*
gazes blissfully into the distance. Birdsong—dawn chorus.

DULLY: Dawn—must be God's own favourite hour of the
twenty-four.
I think so. And the birds seem to think so—they're
bubbling over.
Everything's glittering.
Back at home, the cocks will be stepping in through the

just-opened doorway.

The donkeys will be winding themselves up for the day,
cranking their voices.

The cows will be making a broad dark track through the
dew

Over the silver meadows

Coming to be milked.

And the mountains, the mountains blue beyond
mountains,

Like old drunken sages,

They'll be stretched out in the dew, hazing and sipping.

And my Dad, he'll be singing:

"In good King Charles's golden days

When loyalty no harm meant . . ."

Enter JITTERWIT *in a feverish hurry.*

JITTERWIT: Where's the Master? What's going on? Don't just
sit.

Get everything ready. Isn't he here?

I've had a terrible night, a terrible night!

I want to ask him a vital question. I've got to ask him.

I can't bear it another minute.

DULLY: He's not here yet. What's the matter?

JITTERWIT: I can't bear it. It's terrible!

DULLY: What is?

JITTERWIT: It! It! Oh oaf! When are you going to wake up
to it?

DULLY: If you don't sleep you get sick.

JITTERWIT: Where's Von Gonktop with the telescope?

Enter VON GONKTOP *with an enormous telescope.*

VON GONKTOP: Where's the Master? Isn't he here yet? No?

Are you ready? Is everything ready? Come on, snap to
it.

We can't play about, we're racing against time.

DULLY: I'm always ready, Mr. Von Gonktop.

VON GONKTOP: His great brain's probably got him tied up in some problem. We must be patient. We're lucky he's as patient with us as he is. We're lucky he's taking us with him, do you know that? We're lucky to be sharing the honours.

JITTERWIT: Aren't we going to look through the telescope this morning?

VON GONKTOP: I've already looked.

JITTERWIT: Well?

VON GONKTOP: Worse than ever. Closer than ever. Huger than ever. Now it has a big blue spiky ring round it, like a gigantic flying gas-ring.

JITTERWIT: A blue ring! That wasn't there yesterday.

VON GONKTOP: Yesterday it wasn't as close, was it?
It's travelling at thousands of miles a second
Straight towards us, so it grows.
Closer and closer and closer.
Soon it will be here, it will arrive—
And Bang!—Whoooof!

JITTERWIT: What shall we do? What shall we do? Let me look.
JITTERWIT looks through the telescope, up into the sky.
Enter the MASTER—a bearded scientist.

MASTER: Well, and how is my little meteor this morning?

JITTERWIT: I can't bear to look. It'll turn my hair white!
Master, isn't there any chance . . .

MASTER: Bags packed? Are we ready?

JITTERWIT: Master, can I ask a question?

MASTER: Hurry up, we ought to be off.

JITTERWIT: Can't this meteor possibly miss us? I know it can't, I know your calculations are infallible, but—can't it possibly, just by a hairsbreadth, miss us?

MASTER: Gentlemen, the laws of the Universe are our laws.
If a meteor is hurtling out of the depths of space,
A colossal moon of flying metal

37

In a dazzlingly beautiful blue halo of fire,
Aimed directly at our insignificant earth,
Why, gentlemen, we simply have to accept it.
The Truth is the Truth.

VON GONKTOP: The Truth Is The Truth.

JITTERWIT: Yes, of course. And you know I've given up
everything for the Truth. My home, my job, my friends,
my happiness. . . .

VON GONKTOP: The Master's calculations cannot fail.

MASTER: Out of the question.

VON GONKTOP: The Master has calculated the meteor will
arrive within a few days.

JITTERWIT: Aaaaah!

VON GONKTOP: The Master has calculated that it will shatter
the whole earth and everything on it, within a single
second, into red-hot dust.

JITTERWIT: Aaaaah!

VON GONKTOP: The Master has calculated the exact point of
its first contact with the earth, and we shall be there, to
receive it, if we hurry.

JITTERWIT: The exact point!

MASTER: We are going to stare up into it, unafraid, objective
to the last, observant to the last, scientific to the last,
with our filter-cameras aligned, as it comes smashing
down on to our heads. To the last, we shall be gazing up
into the blazing body of the Truth, as it comes smashing
down on our heads.

JITTERWIT: No!

VON GONKTOP: We are going to face the Truth.

MASTER: We must accept the Truth.

JITTERWIT: Help! We're finished!

   DULLY *falls off his bench. He lies snoring.*

MASTER: We are citizens of the Universe.

VON GONKTOP: We are citizens of the Universe.

38

MASTER: We accept the Universe. Repeat that.

VON GONKTOP *and* JITTERWIT: We accept the Universe.

MASTER [*to* DULLY]: Wake up. We're off.

DULLY: Hmm?

MASTER: Wake up.

DULLY: Eh? What? Where? Oh!

VON GONKTOP: We're off to meet the Truth. You're our porter, so move.

JITTERWIT: The Master is leading us to the Truth. We will follow him to the end.

MASTER: We are noble mankind. Let us not forget it.

JITTERWIT: The Truth! The Truth!

VON GONKTOP: We want the whole Truth.

MASTER: The Absolute Truth.

JITTERWIT: And nothing but the Truth—no, nothing. Yes, yes, yes.

Exeunt these three, shouting these slogans.

DULLY: That's the way they carry on all the time
While I lug their belongings.
They gas about renovating the whole globe
While I cook their grub.
They're wailing about the horrible Nothingness of Outer Space
While I mend their boots.
If you ask me, they're all brains and no sense.
Still, as they say, I'm only an oaf.
Only an oaf, only an oaf,
And I've only got my loaf
To think with.

Re-enter VON GONKTOP, *furious.*

VON GONKTOP: There you are! Idiot! You're holding us back. March!

Exeunt.

GUARDIAN SPIRIT: That is how it begins. And now see what
    follows.
    They travel over mountains, through cities, over seas
    Towards their meeting with the Truth.
    And the whole way the Master spreads his wisdom.
    His two disciples wonder if he is a god
    Walking the earth
    He can work such miracles, so calmly,
    Under the doom of the oncoming meteor
    Which, every day,
    They study carefully through their telescope.
MASTER: It's a pity it's only visible during the day.
    It's probably a fragment of the sun.
    But what a dazzling show it would make in the darkness.
VON GONKTOP: It is definitely getting bigger.
    Now there's a red ring, a hideous inflammation,
    Surrounding the blue ring.
JITTERWIT: I have said good-bye to everything.
    Good-bye to the trees, good-bye to the stones, the water,
    Good-bye to the . . .
MASTER: March! There's still two hundred miles to go.
GUARDIAN SPIRIT: They travel over the desert, through bad
    lands, and through swamps.
    Everywhere the Master spreads his wisdom.
    How does he spread his wisdom?
    And what is his wisdom?
    You shall see his wisdom.
    At last they come to the jungle of red flowers.
    Here, where their meteor is to fall,
    They discover the half-people, who are covered with
    brown fur.
    Wild drumming and singing
MASTER: At last! The spot! This is the very spot
    Where the meteor will first touch our earth,

According to my calculations.

VON GONKTOP: Which are infallible.

MASTER: Nothing could be better.

JITTERWIT: Is this where we're going to be smashed to bits?

MASTER: Set down the bags. Pitch the tents. Gather wood, find
    water.

Get the cooker going.

This is the exact spot.

The dead centre of the meteor is aiming precisely there,

There, where that red flower is, about there.

On this spot

We shall all disappear into the dead centre of the final
    Truth

Smashed to blazing atoms.

VON GONKTOP: The Final Truth!

[JITTERWIT *is sobbing.*]

What's the matter, Jitterwit?

JITTERWIT: I can't bear it.

MASTER: Can't bear what?

JITTERWIT: It's so terrible—everything to go bang! Whooosh!
    Nothing. Not even gravestones.

MASTER: Why, man, even when you drop off in a doze
    It's as bad. Everything finishes.

JITTERWIT: Yes, but then I wake up.

MASTER: And here too you'll wake up. You'll wake up as
    cosmic fire. You'll have been sucked up into the Universe
    like a spoonful of medicine.

What's all that racket?

DULLY: Savages, sir.

MASTER: Savages?

DULLY: They're having a jamboree. They're roasting a
    hippopotamus.

MASTER: It's impossible.

DULLY: What is?

MASTER: There are no savages left. Progress has cleaned up the whole globe. This is the year A.D. 2000. What do they think they're up to?

DULLY: They're savages, sir.

VON GONKTOP: Here, in this tangled jungle, they've been overlooked.

DULLY: They're very special savages, sir.

MASTER: Special? How special?

DULLY: Well, sir, they're covered with brown hair and they have little stumpy tails.

MASTER: Gorillas! Heavens, I've discovered a civilization of gorillas. Gorillas dancing and singing! The gorillas are evolving!

DULLY: No, sir. Not gorillas, people.

MASTER: Well, let's have a closer look at them.

And even though this globe's doomed within days,
Can we let these people carry on in their ignorance?

VON GONKTOP: No. Definitely not.

MASTER: Can we leave them in the misery of their poverty, their diseases, their wretched housing, their appalling diet?

VON GONKTOP: Definitely not.

MASTER: We stand for the advance and happiness of all mankind equally, not excluding even gorillas.

VON GONKTOP: We stand for the advance and happiness of all mankind equally, not excluding even gorillas.

MASTER: Where's my pistol?

[*Fires two shots. Singing and dancing stop.*]

That'll bring them over. Hellooooo!

Remember, tell them nothing about the meteor.

It might make them lose hope before we've had a chance to improve them.

Here they are.

JITTERWIT: Just as you said.

MASTER: Heavens, look at them. They're half-monkeys.
They're covered with brown hair. And look at those
funny little tails.
What a discovery.

CHIEF: White men!

MASTER: They speak.

CHIEF: Friends!

MASTER: And they're friendly. Now these simple people shall
have my help.

GUARDIAN SPIRIT: The Master begins to help the savages.
First, he clears away the forest, burns it to the ground,
So there'll be room for vast crops.
Second, he shoots, poisons and traps all the wild beasts
That might be a danger, with their long fangs and their
hunger.
Third, he destroys all the wild creatures
That might eat the crops.
Fourth, he poisons all the insects
That would infect the crops with their invisible eggs.
Fifth, he poisons all green growth that is not crops,
That might stifle the crops.
And now as far as a man can walk in a day
Like a sea the wheat flows under the wind
Towards the horizon.

MASTER: Meanwhile through space
Every second thousands of miles closer
The meteor rushes with its blazing mouth
To swallow the earth.

JITTERWIT *and* VON GONKTOP, *with telescope.*

VON GONKTOP: Are you still afraid?

JITTERWIT: I've got past being afraid, I think.
I think.
The Master's confidence is a great support.
Yes, I accept the end of everything

If it means the Truth.

VON GONKTOP: The smash should be tremendous.

It will be visible all over the galaxy, probably.

Of course, we shan't see it. We shall be it.

JITTERWIT: How many days now?

VON GONKTOP: A few. The master is working it out exactly.

That's what he's busy at.

JITTERWIT: Great is the Master!

VON GONKTOP: Nothing turns the Master from the Truth.

JITTERWIT: He respects nothing, neither man, woman, nor
child, but the Truth.

VON GONKTOP: Nothing has any Truth for him but the truth.

JITTERWIT: What is the Truth?

VON GONKTOP: There. That is the Truth. Blazing down
towards the earth.

JITTERWIT: Oh, I daren't look. I daren't look any more.

VON GONKTOP: But you must. You must stare the Truth in the
face.

JITTERWIT *looks*.

JITTERWIT: Now there's a purple ring round the red ring.

A blue ring, a red ring, a purple ring
Like a terrific target.

We're the target! I can't look.

Enter CHIEF *of savages*.

CHIEF: Hail!

VON GONKTOP: Ah, Chief Ugglamuggla, what's the news?

CHIEF: Where is the Master?

VON GONKTOP: What's the matter, you're in a sweat.

CHIEF: Where is the Master?

VON GONKTOP: Please don't look so fierce. He's in his tent.

But don't disturb him, he's deep in calculation.

CHIEF: I must speak with the Master, quick.

VON GONKTOP: Come back. Don't disturb him.

He is calculating the date of the arrival of the truth.

CHIEF: Our wheat is on fire. All the horizons are blazing.
All our food has gone up in smoke. Master!
All run out.
DULLY: Now the entire landscape is black ashes.
The savages have no more food,
Except what they'd dried and preserved from the earlier days
When it grew on the trees.
There is no jungle fruit now, the Master cleared all the jungle.
There are no game animals, he poisoned them all.
There is nothing on the plains but a hot wind
Carrying ashes.
But the Master has a solution.
He sends for machines.
The savages will make motor-cars.
He has them building factories, to make motor-cars.
The savages will send their motor-cars abroad,
And in payment they will get food back.
The savages set to work, because they are hungry.
If you ask me, this is a great disaster
For these savages. Here they come
Carrying spades to dig foundations
Of the factories.
SAVAGES *go over the stage, carrying spades.* OVERSEER *goads them on.*
OVERSEER: Get along there. Sweat. Work. If you don't want to starve
Get moving. The factories have to be built.
They're our one chance. Factories have to be built
To build the motor-cars to buy the bread.
Get a move on.
FIRST SAVAGE: When will the bread be here? Our families are hungry.

SECOND SAVAGE: Our chief has grown cruel.
    He drives us to dig foundations.
    When we tire, he beats us.
OVERSEER: Fools, if you don't dig there'll be no bread.
    Both you and he will starve. And me, too. Move.
DULLY: Now the motor-cars are driving
    Off the production line.
    The master has made everything go like magic
    With his great brain.
    Now the first consignment of motor-cars
    Drives away, to be loaded on to ships, at the port.
    Soon, says the Master, soon now bread will be coming
    With other tasty titbits.
ALL: Bread, bread, we want bread.
    We've built the motor-cars, where is the bread?
ONE SAVAGE: Where are the hippos and the paw-paw fruit?
ALL: Bread, bread, we want bread.
    We've built the motor-cars, where is the bread?
TWO SAVAGES: Our families are starving.
    Wailing of the families.
ALL: Our families are starving.
DULLY: Now they refuse to build more motor-cars
    Till they get bread. They down tools.
OVERSEER: Work. Work. Work.
ALL: Bread. Bread. Bread. Bread. Bread. Bread. We want
    bread.
    This goes on in background.
CHIEF: Listen to my people.
MASTER: Their distress is understandable.
    Tell them bread is coming, shiploads of it.
    To pay for the lovely motor-cars they built.
    But they must not stop building motor-cars
    To buy yet more bread after that bread's finished.
    When they stop building motor-cars, they starve.

46

Tell them that.

CHIEF: I will tell them.

CHIEF goes.

MASTER: These wretched savages certainly are unlucky.

Who would have thought their wheatfields would catch fire,

Leaving them foodless. Yet what does it matter?

In exactly an hour, the meteor arrives,

Lands on our skulls and smashes the globe to bits.

That will solve their problems, thank goodness.

I have calculated the exact second.

I'll go and prepare the cameras.

Exit, as JITTERWIT *wanders in.*

JITTERWIT: Did you hear that? In an hour.

DULLY: What's the matter, Mr. Jitterwit?

JITTERWIT: We're finished! One more hour and everything's finished.

DULLY: Don't you take it so hard.

JITTERWIT: The Master has made his calculations, it's all tied up.

DULLY: Don't you take it to heart.

JITTERWIT: Oaf! You don't understand!

DULLY: Well, I know I'm an oaf, but your master seems a bit stupid to me, making all this fuss.

JITTERWIT: Stupid? Do you know what you're saying?

He's the most famous man on earth at the moment.

DULLY: But all this rubbish about a meteor!

JITTERWIT: But that's exactly it. You could almost call it his meteor.

He's calculated the speed, the weight,

The exact point and moment

At which it will strike. And it's right here, in an hour.

DULLY: Don't get worked up.

JITTERWIT: I don't want to die. I don't want the world

47

To be blasted to bits. I like it.

Why shouldn't I get worked up?

DULLY: Well, I can't see this meteor.

JITTERWIT: Have you looked through the telescope?

It's a blazing golden ball

With a fierce blue circle around it

And around that circle, a fierce red bigger circle,

And around that one, a fierce purple circle—

It's rushing to swallow us up, bigger every minute.

DULLY: Show me.

JITTERWIT: Look, imbecile, look.

DULLY: Ah, yes.

JITTERWIT: Ah yes, he says. Aren't you scared out of your wits?

What are you doing? What are you doing?

Unscrewing the telescope?

DULLY: Well, look. There's your meteor

Inside the telescope.

JITTERWIT: Aaaaaah!

DULLY: It's a spot of fungus growing on the lens.

A spot of lurid mould. You see, yellow-centre,

Then a blue ring, then a red, then a purple—

It must be growing quite fast in this climate.

JITTERWIT: Ooooh! It's a blot of penicillin!

Our meteor's nothing but a spot of fungus!

The master's been deceived by a mushroom!

Enter at great speed VON GONKTOP.

VON GONKTOP: Pack the bags. Strike camp. Run for your lives.

A messenger has just arrived.

The whole shipload of motor-cars

Was sunk at sea by commercial pirates. The savages are
    rising.

Wild drumming and yelling, off.

Enter the MASTER *at great speed.*

MASTER: Was it my fault? Can I control the seas?

They'd have become rich. They'd have become
A flourishing modern industrial society
Within a few years. They've done everything wrong.
They have no patience. They cannot listen to sense.
Civilization has taught them nothing.
Now their cars are sunk at sea and all their land is ruined.
Run, drop everything and run.
They're going to eat us. They're suddenly cannibals.
There's nothing left for them but to eat us.
All run off. Drums and wild yells louder.

GUARDIAN SPIRIT: The master and his disciples and the Porter
    Run for their lives
    Across the blackened plains. They escape
    Back to civilization.
    They have cleaned the telescope.
    And though they can no longer see any meteor
    Their confidence is restored,
    For now the lens is clean.
MASTER: We shall not make the same mistake again.
VON GONKTOP: And we reacted to what we thought was the
    world's end
    In the very noblest way. We marched to meet it.
JITTERWIT: We are proud of ourselves.
MASTER: We acted sensibly and very nobly
    And, to the last, like true scientists.
    We pursued what we thought was the truth, and nothing
    stopped us, nothing.
    Only our thoughts were mistaken,
    For we are merely men.
VON GONKTOP: And man is full of error.
MASTER: Man is himself an error.
    Only the Truth can make man greater than man,

Can make him the Truth.

DULLY: And so we wandered the world.
And everywhere we went
The master spread his wisdom.
And everywhere he spread his wisdom
The lands blackened, the wind blew hot with ashes,
And men were plunged in discontent,
Misery and deprivation.
And motor-car factories arose to make them happy.
Did the motor-car factories make men happy?
Or if not motor-car factories, canning factories.
Did canning factories make men happy?
Or if not canning factories,
Mental hospitals,
And beside the mental hospitals,
Hospitals.
And beside the hospitals,
Crematoriums.

But there was one thing the master could not do.
He could not make the dead live.
He could not turn the dead into the living.
Nor where he had created a desolation
Could he create grass.

MASTER: What good is all my wisdom?
What good is all my mastery of the laws
Of creation? I cannot create life.

DULLY: The problem kept him awake.
He beat his brains on his books, on his formulae.
And at last he thought he almost had it.
And at that moment he heard of a wise man
Who lived on a remote mountain
Who could revive the dead. He could make the dead live
So ran the rumour,

And out of the dead stone he could bring grass.

MASTER: A man wiser than I am? Impossible!
Let him test his knowledge against mine.
He can revive the dead? Impossible!
So could I, if I were really put to the test.
Let him test his wisdom against mine
We'll expose this faker.

VON GONKTOP: No man is wiser than the Master.
No man has greater knowledge
Of the mysteries of creation
Than the Master.

JITTERWIT: Praise him! Praise Him!

VON GONKTOP: You could make the dead live, if you really tried.
You have not really tried.

MASTER: Yes, I believe I could.

VON GONKTOP: You have never truly tested yourself.

MASTER: Eureka!

JITTERWIT: What? What is it?

MASTER: I can raise the dead. I say I can.
[*Both cheer.*]
I will test my powers against this man.

DULLY: Once more we grew blisters inside our boots,
Stumbling over the wastelands of this world.
We came to the mountains, the blue tepees of the gods.
I am a simple man, I believe in gods.
We climbed, where wild goats leaned out
Over gulfs full of the whisper of torrents
And gunfire of landslides. We climbed
Where eagles slid from us and hung out
Over a five-mile drop into forest.
We climbed. We climbed till our brains altered
And we could see mountains upside down
On top of the mountains. We saw smoke like horsehair
   stuffing

Belching out of a crevice between stones.
When we got closer, there was no smoke. Nothing
But a solitary blue mountain flower, the size of a shirt-
button.
Then we heard a tremendous klaxon voice announcing
the winner
That suddenly stopped. Later, a woman's head sank
from the air
Floating between us, waist-high, smiling at us,
And gliding on down the mountain. We climbed
Till we came to a cave.
I can tell you, it was hard going. In front of the cave
An ancient man was sitting, watching us climb.
The hair and beard of a goat, and decorated
With feathers and talons of eagles.

MASTER: Good day, sir. I said, Good day, sir.
VON GONKTOP: He doesn't seem to see or hear
Even though we've got so near.
MASTER: I said: Good day, sir.
SAGE: So you've come.
MASTER: Of course I've come. Why, did you expect me?
SAGE: Of course I expected you.
MASTER: Hm! How? Rumours, I suppose.
SAGE: You are the first human beings
To have trod this slope.
MASTER: Ha-hah. Then you must know why I've come, if
you're a thought reader.
SAGE: Of course.
MASTER: Hmm!
VON GONKTOP: Watch him, Master, he's going to pull a fast
one.
JITTERWIT: If he pulls a fast one, it will be his last one.
MASTER: This is Von Gonktop, Research Assistant.
SAGE: Greetings.

MASTER: This is Mr. Jitterwit, Laboratory Attendant.

SAGE: Greetings. And what is the name of your leader?

MASTER: Me. I'm the leader. The whole world knows me as
the Master.

I have given up my private name.

SAGE: But who is that fourth one, your leader?

VON GONKTOP: Look out, I think he's needling us.

JITTERWIT: The ugly, scruffy, whiskery cuss!

MASTER: The fourth? There are only three of us.

SAGE: I see four.

MASTER: O, him. He's only the porter. He's just the man.

SAGE: So he is your leader!

MASTER: He is not! I am! Impudence!

SAGE: Greetings and blessings, wise one.

DULLY: Who, me? I thank you, sir. And a good day to you, sir,
too.

MASTER: Impudence!

VON GONKTOP: Look at the rascal's dirty dhoti.

JITTERWIT: He's certainly lousy and probably potty.

MASTER: Wait a minute. Do you know who I am?

SAGE: Of course.

MASTER: You know what I've done?

SAGE: Of course.

MASTER: You know I am called the Wisest Man In The World.

SAGE: And I know the Dog is called the dog
And I know the Mud is called the mud.

VON GONKTOP: Did you hear what he said?

JITTERWIT: Crack him over the head.

MASTER: Sir, I suspect you are mocking me.

SAGE: Then come to the point.

MASTER: I challenge you to a test of mental strength.
Do you accept or don't you? If you don't
Then I take it I've won.

SAGE: You see those bones scattered among the rocks?

53

MASTER: Those are the bones of a tiger.
An unusually large specimen.
SAGE: Correct.
I can assemble the bones of that tiger
With a single word.
MASTER: With only a word? But that's absurd.
SAGE: Agagagagagagaga!
MASTER: Haha! So much for that. Nothing.
SAGE: Agagagagagagagaga!
JITTERWIT: They moved!
SAGE: Agagagagagagagagagagagagagagagagagaga
As he goes on, the others say
JITTERWIT: They're moving.
VON GONKTOP: It's astounding. They're bounding together
like rats and mice.
MASTER: Hmmm!
VON GONKTOP: He's done it.
SAGE *is silent.*
MASTER: A very crafty trick!
A perfectly assembled skeleton. Congratulations.
I suppose, though, that's the limit of your powers?
SAGE: I can put flesh and blood and skin on to the bones
With a single word.
MASTER: I'd like to see that! That I cannot believe!
JITTERWIT: He's pretty slick!
VON GONKTOP: It's just a trick.
SAGE: I drape my tiger skin over the skeleton: so.
MASTER: Well, go ahead.
SAGE: Gohogogogogogogogogogogogogogogogogogogog!
MASTER: Nothing yet, is there?
SAGE: Gohogogogogogogogogogogogogogogogogog!
JITTERWIT: It moved. I saw it. It moved.
SAGE: Gohogogogogogogogogogogogogogogogogogogogogo-
gogogog

He goes on.

DULLY: Look out, Master, look out.

VON GONKTOP: A tiger! A tiger!

MASTER: Heavens! My word and goodness gracious!

He's actually done it. Dear me, dear me.

This is going to be difficult, I can see.

[SAGE *is now silent.*]

But is this tiger dead or living?

DULLY: If it's living, let's be leaving.

SAGE: Alas, this glorious tiger, perfect as it is

In every anatomical detail, is dead.

MASTER: So then your powers are not such a great wonder.

It was mainly bragging and propaganda.

You've no real thunderbolts, you've just got thunder.

SAGE: Alas, there are limits to my powers.

MASTER: But I heard you could revive the dead

And set them jumping for meat and bread.

SAGE: Untrue.

MASTER: Well, I can. I can revive the dead.

I will bring life back into this tiger.

Porter, pass the bag of instruments.

DULLY: Master, be careful.

MASTER: Pass it. The hypodermic syringe.

DULLY: But, Master, this is a tiger—if you can revive it—

VON GONKTOP: Praise the Master's wisdom, he can revive the
dead.

JITTERWIT: He can set them howling for meat and bread.

VON GONKTOP: He can set them leaping higher than your head.

BOTH: Praise him! Praise him! Praise him!

We have given our lives into the keeping of his wisdom.

MASTER: We call this little magic wand a hypodermic syringe.

I shall just jab this needle into the tiger——

DULLY: Wait, wait.

MASTER: What?

55

DULLY: Please just give me time to squeeze myself
   Into the top of that solitary, straggly thorn tree.
MASTER: What, are you afraid?
VON GONKTOP: Coward!
JITTERNIT: Coward!
VON GONKTOP: Run from progress.
JITTERWIT: Run in fear from the mighty achievements of man.
DULLY: Yes, oh yes, I'm a coward when it comes to tigers
   That haven't had a bite for many a year.
   Exit DULLY.
MASTER: Behold, I stick this needle into the tiger.
DULLY [*off*]: Good-bye.
MASTER: And I inject. Rise, tiger, awake:
   Lift up thy body and walk.
   [*Terrific roar of a tiger.*]
   I've done it! I've done it!
JITTERWIT *and* VON GONKTOP: Hip, Hip, Hooray.
 Hip hip hoor—AAAAAAAAAAAAAaaaaaaaaaaahhhh!
   All scream. Horrible roar.
   Roar upon roar. Their screams die.
   Long silence.
DULLY: The tiger ate them all.
   The tiger ate the Master, hair and fingernails and all.
   The tiger ate them all.
   The tiger ate Von Gonktop from his big toe to his eye-ball.
   The tiger ate them all.
   The tiger ate poor Jitterwit, and it ground his bones up
      small.
   The tiger ate them all.

   But isn't it strange.
   The moment the tiger jumped to its feet
   The whiskery old man vanished—just disappeared.
   Pop—gone, like a bubble.

And there was only a tiger, swallowing my comrades.
So now I'm going home, none the wiser.
I'll have to think of a moral to this story.

GUARDIAN SPIRIT: So the porter returns to his father's farm.
Where the cockerels shake their metals
And the donkeys crank their voices
And the cows sway, heavier than tubs of butter,
And the mountains say nothing
But stay as they are, stretched full length in the sun,
Smoking idly, gazing up into the blue.
And the farmer, strolling around his boundary, sings:

DULLY: In good King Charles's golden days
When loyalty no harm meant. . . .

Beauty and the Beast

Characters

THE FLOORSWEEPER
THE FATHER
HIS SON
HIS DAUGHTER FLOREAT
THE DOCTOR
THE BEARKEEPER
THE BEAR

Beauty and the Beast

Enter FLOORSWEEPER.

FLOORSWEEPER: I don't know what's going on in this house,
    I don't.
It's all very funny. And not very nice.
The master is a millionaire
But that doesn't help him.
Something's mysteriously wrong with his daughter.
Something's wrong with his daughter and he dotes on her.
What good are his millions, his yachts, his Rolls,
His thousands of acres crawling with leopards and
    peacocks,
None of it can help her.
She just gets paler and paler.
He can't sign a cheque to put some colour in her cheeks.
But what's wrong with his daughter?

Enter FATHER *and* SON.

FATHER: This is the eighth doctor.

SON: He's probably no good either.

FATHER: Was she screaming last night?

SON: She woke me three times, Father.

FATHER: Do you know what I'm suspecting?

SON: Don't tell me you think it's witchcraft.

FATHER: Witchcraft. Yes, witchcraft.

SON: Witchcraft doesn't exist.

FATHER: Doctors peer under her eyelids, finger her pulses,
　　　Listen to her lungs, study her blood,
　　　Diet her on parsley, then on salami,
　　　Then make her fast on water. They're useless.
　　　There's nothing wrong with her body.
　　　It's all in her mind. She's bewitched.
SON: It's beyond me, anyway.
FATHER: The doctor's whispering in there with her.
SON: That'll be another bill as long as a dog-chain
　　　With some dreadful figure snarling at the end of it.
FATHER: Money! Money! Why, money's nothing
　　　If they can cure her. If they could make her smile.
　　　She's just lost interest in everything.
　　　If they could make her smile, that would be something.
SON: Maybe a laugh would jerk her out of it.
FATHER: Maybe you're right. Maybe a laugh would do it.
　　　[*Enter* DOCTOR, *leading the daughter*, FLOREAT.]
　　　Here she is. Now, how are you this morning?
DOCTOR: Shhhh! Keep off. Don't disturb her.
　　　What are all these people crowding here for?
FATHER: These are my family, my servants, my men—
　　　They love my daughter, they've come to show their
　　　　concern.
DOCTOR: She must be left alone. Kept quiet.
　　　Given soft music. She must not be crowded and stared at.
SON: Nonsense. Come on, let's make her laugh.
　　　All she needs is some merriment.
　　　Hahahahahahaha!
　　　All laugh, prolonged laughter. FLOREAT *grows sadder.*
DOCTOR: Stop! Stop! STOP!
　　　[*Laughter dies.*]
　　　You'll send her crazy. Are you crazy?
SON: Well, it didn't help much, for sure, did it?
DOCTOR: Now all of you leave.

FATHER: Wait. Now, Floreat, my little mouse,
    What do you want? Shall we go yachting?
    [*She shakes her head.*]
    Fishing for bonito, in the Gulf of Mexico?
    [*She shakes her head.*]
    Shall we go hunting gazelles, in Arabia, with cheetahs?
    [*She shakes her head.*]
    How about some gliding in the Alps?
    [*She shakes her head.*]
    How about some gambling? Blow in a million.
    That should get your circulation going.
    [*She shakes her head.*]
    How about a tour through Baluchistan?
    You could get some carpets for your room.
FLOREAT: Nothing! I don't want anything. Leave me alone.
DOCTOR: You see? Now, if you please, all of you, leave.
FATHER: You know the reward, Doctor, if you cure her.
SON: What she needs is entertainment
    Of a surprising sort. Something lively.
FATHER: Everybody out.
    All exeunt, except DOCTOR *and* FLOREAT.
DOCTOR: Now, my girl, tell me just what's wrong.
    Describe it to me.
FLOREAT: It's horrible.
DOCTOR: Describe it. I can't cure it till you describe it.
FLOREAT: It's too horrible.
DOCTOR: Nothing's that horrible. Now, it comes over you
    after dark. Is that right?
FLOREAT: Yes.
DOCTOR: While you're asleep?
FLOREAT: Yes.
DOCTOR: And what does it look like? Hm?
FLOREAT: I daren't think.
DOCTOR: Well, is it—er—a ghost?

63

FLOREAT: No, not quite.

DOCTOR: Not quite! Is it a bird?

FLOREAT: No.

DOCTOR: Do you see it?

FLOREAT: No.

DOCTOR: Hm! Do you hear it?

FLOREAT: Yes.

DOCTOR: And what sound does it make?

FLOREAT: No!

DOCTOR: No what?

FLOREAT [*screams*]: I can't bear to think of it.

She begins to wail and cry. Enter FATHER.

FATHER: What's going on? What are you doing to her?

DOCTOR: Shhh! Will you please leave us alone.

I was just getting to it.

FATHER: Have a care, Doctor. Nothing too drastic.

Her nerves are not too strong.

DOCTOR: Yes, well, I think she'd better rest.

I think she'd better go back to bed for a while.

She's missing her sleep. Perhaps she could snatch some
sleep,

While I'm thinking of a cure.

FATHER: Back to bed, Floreat. Get some sleep.

[*Exit* FLOREAT.]

Well, what have you discovered?

DOCTOR: Nothing—except there's something.

FATHER: We knew that. We don't need to finance a doctor

To be told that. I can tell you more.

It's something so hideous no woman

Will stay the night with her. They come out screaming.

But they don't know what's frightened them either.

DOCTOR: Hm! Most mysterious!

FATHER: Is it a demon? Is she haunted by a demon

Like Sarah, in the book of Tobit?

64

A terrible, man-killing demon? Or what?

DOCTOR: I have an idea.

FATHER: We need one.

DOCTOR: Tonight, I'll hide under her bed.

FATHER: Hm!

DOCTOR: If it's something outside her own brain—
Why, I shall see it. Or hear it.
I shall feel it anyway. I shall have met it.
I doubt if it will drive me out screaming.
Maybe then I can treat it.

FATHER: Good. I like it. Do it. Tonight.

DOCTOR: Tonight it is.

Exeunt. Enter FLOORSWEEPER.

FLOORSWEEPER: I don't like the looks of this at all.
The poor girl gets whiter and whiter.
Her eyes are droopy weepy
Or else dry and staring.
And this doctor's an idiot.
All doctors are a sort of idiot, if you ask me.
They're so smart, they become idiots.
Now he's hiding under her bed
To catch her ailment red-handed.
Every month it's a new one.
Well, she breaks my heart
To have such idiots gambolling around her
When she's so sick.

Exit. FLOREAT *climbs into bed. Enter* DOCTOR.

DOCTOR: There she lies on her bed. She falls asleep readily
To say she has such nightmares waiting for her.
If I creep out of sight here under her bed . . .
[*He creeps under the bed.*]
Now, whatever it is, coming to get her,
Let it come. I'm ready for it. Shhhhh! Listen.

FLOREAT [*softly*]: Ooooooh!

DOCTOR: Is she asleep?

He peers out.

FLOREAT [*louder*]: Oooooooh!

DOCTOR: Something's coming. Something's here. What is it?

Loud steady banging.

TREMENDOUS VOICE: Let me in. Let me in. I've come for you.

FLOREAT [*almost a cry*]: Ooooooh!

Bangings grow louder and more violent, seem to come first from one side then from the other, and the voice, louder and closer, seems likewise to come from all sides.

VOICE: I've come for you. Awake and let me in.

I'm coming to get you. Awake and open the doors.

DOCTOR *jumps out.*

DOCTOR: Get away, whatever you are, get away, out of it!

[*He bangs the fire-irons, etc., together.*]

Help! Help! Help!

FLOREAT *wakes, begins to scream.*

Door bursts open, enter FATHER *and* SON *in nightshirts.*

FATHER: What's going on? Hello? Hello? Hello?

FLOREAT: Daddy!

FATHER: It's all right, my little love, it's me.

SON: What was it?

FATHER: Where is it?

SON: Did you see it?

DOCTOR: It's gone.

Exeunt. Enter FLOORSWEEPER.

FLOORSWEEPER: Well, what was it? I just wonder.

If you ask me, this place is fearfully haunted.

It's a revenge from heaven, for her father being so rich,

It's sinful to be so rich. It makes you stupid.

And maybe this is his punishment.

That frightened me last night, and I don't mind saying it.

Why, my hair stood on end, right up on end,

And I'm at the top of the house, in the attics.

66

The poor old dog must have heard it, he's still trembling.
He's jammed himself right back under the stove
And won't come out. He's still in there, whining.
The cats have disappeared, they've run off into the woods.
There are no sparrows in the yard. And all morning
I haven't seen a single cockroach or fly.
Everything's terrified and gone.
Everything's shunning this house.
Enter FATHER *and* DOCTOR.
FATHER: Tonight, I'll watch with you.
DOCTOR: Ah, it was horrible!
FATHER: So you keep saying. Describe it, exactly.
DOCTOR: It was—I can't quite say—it was—
Horrible! Horrible!
FATHER: Hm! It seems to have been alarming all right.
But it won't frighten me out of action.
I shall bring along my pistols.
I'm something of an expert, you know,
At shooting trout through the head when they jump for
flies,
Or driving a nail in at fifty paces.
DOCTOR: I saw nothing to shoot at.
FATHER: Still shaken?
DOCTOR: My mouth tastes ghastly, like an old shoe.
FATHER: That's fear.
DOCTOR: I'll wait in her room with you, nevertheless.
We must run this monster to earth.
FATHER: A monster, you call it.
DOCTOR: What else can we call it?
FATHER: How is she?
DOCTOR: Today she's bad. Lying in bed.
She really hasn't the strength to move, not after last night.
FATHER: If we don't act tonight. I'm afraid
We shall be too late.

DOCTOR: I am with you.

FLOORSWEEPER *in her nightgown.*

FLOORSWEEPER: I'm not going to sleep tonight.

I'm going to bed with a poker.

The doctor and her father are fully armed.

Her brother has been practising with his twelve bore.

The doctor and her father are under her bed.

The brother is walking round and round the house.

Eleven's already struck. There's no moon.

Will it come tonight?

There's not a breath of wind on the trees.

Will it stir? Will it come? What's that?

Enter SON.

SON: What are you doing here?

FLOORSWEEPER: Just going to bed, sir. It's a dark stair up to my room, sir,

I was just screwing up courage.

After last night, sir.

SON: Get up with you, it's nothing but my sister's nightmares.

FLOORSWEEPER: Oh, sir, you haven't seen the dog, how he's taken it.

SON: The dog?

FLOORSWEEPER: Or the cat.

SON: Why, what have they got to do with it?

FLOORSWEEPER: If I die of fright tonight, it won't be my fault.

SON: Silly old woman!

SON *goes off whistling, she goes.*

DOCTOR *and* FATHER *peer from under* FLOREAT'S *bed.*

DOCTOR: Now's the time. Listen.

FATHER: There's not much room under this bed for manœuvres.

DOCTOR: Shhhhh!

Twelve strikes.

FATHER: Not a sound. It's an unusually still night.

DOCTOR: Shhh!

68

FLOREAT [*muffled*]: Oooooh! No! No!

FATHER: Is that Floreat? Floreat—are you all right?

DOCTOR: Shhhh! Let it come. Be still.

Wind rises. Wind sounds increasing.

FATHER: The wind's getting up. Something's getting up.

DOCTOR: See that—lightning.

Thunder.

TREMENDOUS VOICE: I have come for you.

FLOREAT: Help! Help!

Thunder.

TREMENDOUS VOICE: I am coming in to get you! This time I
shall get you!

DOCTOR: Here it comes again.

FATHER: It's an earthquake. This is an earthquake,
The house is rocking.

TREMENDOUS VOICE: Now you will be mine.

Thunder. FLOREAT *cries loud.*

DOCTOR: Look out. The wall's cracking open. It's an earthquake.

FATHER: There it is. Look. There. Look.

[*He fires twice.*

Thunder.

Loud agonized wail goes off into the distance.

Wind dies.

Silence.]

I got him. I'm certain I got him.

Enter SON.

SON: What is it? Where is it?

FATHER: I got him. It's all right, my darling,
Your dad's here and I've killed the monster.

SON: What happened? I didn't see a thing.

FATHER: Where's the doctor?

SON: Here, under the bed.

FATHER: It's all right. You can come out. We've won.
Drag him out.

son: Look at him, his hair's gone white.
It was black and it's gone snow white.
father: That's fear for you. That's real terror for you.
doctor: Oh, I thought it was the end of the world.
father: I saw a giant figure in the gap.
The walls were cracking open and this figure
Was tearing the crack wider and shoving in—
I fired twice, dead centre. I don't think I missed.
We're going to need the builders.
son: No trace of him.
father: Yes, there's blood, see it,
On the mirror, still dripping.
son: And here's a spot of it on this powder compact.
father: It's all right, Floreat, I got him.
son: There's no body. He must have crawled away.
doctor: Well, that settles one thing.
father: What?
doctor: It's not just in her mind, is it?
son: And it's wounded.
floorsweeper: Three nights now and nothing's happened.
They say the monster has died in the forest.
Her father fired his pistol into its body.
But his daughter's no better.
If you ask me, she's worse.
But now the son's having a go, and they've sent the doctor
packing.
He's glad to be going.
That night aged him ten years.
But now her brother's found her some amusement.
He's convinced that if she could laugh, she'd be cured.
So he's found her something amusing. Well, we'll see.
Enter son.
son: He's here. He's coming. Where's Floreat? Where is she?
Here comes the bearkeeper. Here comes the dancing Bear.

70

What a bear!
Black as the gullet of a chimney,
With claws like garden forks,
But he dances like a joker.
Enter FATHER.

FATHER: Are you sure it's not a dangerous bear?
Bears are notorious, they're shiftier than the weather.
Every bear has two demons.
One for plaguing himself, one for plaguing the world.
When he strokes you, your arms fall off.
Pipes. Enter BEARKEEPER *with* BEAR.

SON: What's wrong with your bear? What's that bandage?
Has he been hurt?

BEARKEEPER: Good morning, good morning, ladies and
    gentlemen.
First, I will explain this slight imperfection in my bear.
A little accident, a teeny accident.
An imbecile bird-hunter in the forest.
My Bonzo—his majesty the bear
Is called Bonzo—has a pet canary. Yes,
He's so clever and tame, he keeps a canary.
Believe it or not. They are great friends,
Him and his pet canary.

FATHER: And what happened?

BEARKEEPER: Why, my Bonzo was playing with his pet.
He held up his paws, and the canary
Sat on his talon, pecking seeds from his lips.
We were sitting having our lunch in the forest.
The bird-hunter was creeping among the ferns.
He saw the bobbing yellow of the canary.
He did not see the burly black of Bonzo.
He thought Bonzo was the hairy bole of a yew tree
Where the canary was sitting. He fired. And he missed.
He hit my Bonzo's paw. Didn't he, Bonzo?

BONZO *roars.*

FATHER: Shouldn't you have him on a chain?

BEARKEEPER: Bonzo on a chain! Sacrilege!

SON: But maybe the wound's upset his temper a little.

BEARKEEPER: Look, I put my hand into his gullet.
And now—look. See him licking my throat?
Now—look—he hugs me. Love me, Bonzo.

SON: Look out, he'll squash you like a tube of tooth-paste.

BEARKEEPER: No, no, no, he's very, very gentle.
See him licking my ear.

FATHER: That's amazing!

SON: Floreat, come and see the wonderful bear.
Enter FLOREAT.

FLOREAT: Oh, what a lovely beast!

FATHER: Ah, well. At least she likes something.
That's a start.

SON: Now make him dance and be comical.

BEARKEEPER: Stand back. Are you ready? Dance, Bonzo,
dance.
He pipes, the BEAR *dances.*

FATHER: Extraordinary! Amazing! Staggering! Stupendous!

SON: Look at Floreat, she's smiling.
Piping stops.

FATHER: How much for your bear? I'll buy him.

BEARKEEPER: Sorry, sir, Bonzo could never leave me.

FATHER: I'll buy you both. How much for the two of you?

FLOREAT: Yes. Let me dance, I want to dance with the bear.

FATHER: Floreat, no.

FLOREAT: I want to, I want to, he can hold one end
Of my ribbon and I'll hold the other.

BEARKEEPER: O he'll do that. He's very very clever,
And very gentle.

SON: Let her, Father. Look at her. She's happy.
Piping. BEAR *and* FLOREAT *dance.*

72

FATHER: Where's my camera? I must go get my camera.
This is the shot of a lifetime.
He runs out. BEAR *picks up* FLOREAT *and runs out.* FLOREAT
screams.
SON: Stop! Stop! Father! The bear's got Floreat.
The bear's running away with her.
Come back. Fetch my guns, somebody.
He's picked her up like a baby. He's snatched her.
Help.
He runs out. FATHER *runs in.*
FATHER: What? Which way? Which way did they go?
Where've they gone? What's happened?
SON [*off*]: This way. The bear's galloping into the forest,
Over the fields and into the forest
And Floreat's under his arm.
FATHER: It's the monster. The monster in the likeness of a bear!
He's tricked us. The monster's got my daughter.
Exeunt.
FLOORSWEEPER: Three days now that she's been gone
Under the bear's arm. What is she by now?
The bear would polish her off in a couple of hours.
He'd crunch her bones on the second day.
He'd chew her slippers and swallow them on the third.
Bears eat everything.
Her father is wild. He's combing the land with dogs.
Her brother has sworn to skin it and nail the skin
To the floor of the hallway, where all wipe their feet.
But I think it's hopeless.
The bear's devoured her by now, and gone away
Over the mountain, to yawn in the next country.
Bears are wise, even the horrible ones.
All the hunters will come back with is sorrow.
BEAR *and* FLOREAT *in cave.*
FLOREAT: Why are you keeping me in this cave?

73

I've counted three nights. Why are you keeping me?
Eat me and have done with it.
[BEAR *growls.*]
It's strange, but you seem to be a gentle bear.
Was it really you who came at night
Those other times? And did my father wound you?
[BEAR *growls.*]
You spoke then. Why can't you speak now?
[BEAR *growls.*]
Let me look at your bandage.
But you look ferocious. Your eyes are the eyes
That gloat into the smoking insides of a cow
When you've torn it open.
[BEAR *growls angrily.*]
And your enormous talons. What are they for,
But for digging rabbits out of the earth,
Or the hearts out of men?
[BEAR *growls angrily.*]
And why are you so black? And so huge!
You are so prodigiously ugly!
If you are going to eat me eat me quickly.
[*She begins to sob.* BEAR *growls.*]
What are these? Bilberries again?
Have you brought me bilberries again?
And blackberries? And raspberries?
And wild watercress? And apples?
You're a mysteriously kind bear.
[BEAR *growls angrily.*]
What? What's the matter?
[*Yelping of hounds.*]
Hounds! The hunters! The hunters are coming.
They must have found your track.
It must be my father and the hunters.
[BEAR *growls.*]

Come back. They'll kill you. They'll kill you. O he's gone.
They'll kill him if they see him.
[*Hounds now yelping close.*]
Why has he brought me here?
Why is he so kind to me?
Does he think I'm a bear?
For three days now he's fed me,
And watched me, and not once
Frightened me. Why? Why?
Why didn't he devour me?
Why did he bother to bring me?
Is he lonely here?
Now they're going to kill him.
To free me, they will kill him.
They will kill my bear.
I must stop them. Come back.
Gunshots. BEAR *roars. Hounds yelp.*
FATHER: I got him! I got him!
Enter the BEAR.
FLOREAT: Have they hit you? O you're bleeding.
[*She runs to cave mouth.*]
Stop! Stop shooting!
SON: Look, that must be its mate. A white bear. Shoot.
Shoot it for its valuable skin.
Shots.
FLOREAT: Stop shooting. It's me. Floreat.
FATHER: Stop shooting. Stop shooting.
[*He comes up.*]
It's you! Floreat! You're still alive!
FLOREAT: Of course I am! The bear fed me. He loves me
And I love him. Stop shooting, you've hurt him.
FATHER: What are you babbling about?
SON: The strain must have cracked her wits. She's loony.
FATHER: Pass me the heavy gun, I'll go in there

75

And finish off that monster.

FLOREAT: Stop, stop, stop!
    The bear's fed me. Look at me.
    I'm better. I'm happy. I'm cured.
    Please stop and hear me.

FATHER: Floreat, what's going on?

SON: Who's that there in the cave, that young man?
    Enter, from cave, youth carrying a bear's head and skin.

YOUTH: Will you let me explain?
    There's a strange story to be told.

FLOREAT: O you're bleeding.

YOUTH: The bullet's broken my arm.
    I am the bear. I am the monster in the night.
    Give your belief time. For fifteen years
    I have been a bear in the sight of men and women.
    At all other times, a flying dragon.
    I would have been a bear and a flying dragon
    To the end of my days
    If Floreat had never said she loved me.

FLOREAT: Loved you!

YOUTH: Those were the words I needed to break the spell.

SON: But who was the bearkeeper?

YOUTH: He was illusion.
    I made you think you saw him. He was not there.
    This is the skin and the head of the bear that I was.
    This is the hole of the bullet you fired at the bear,
    Here in my arm.

FLOREAT: He's fainting. He's losing all that blood.

FATHER: Men, help him. Bring him along. We'll hear this story.

SON: He's a remarkably handsome fellow, for a bear.

FLOREAT: Take him gently, gently.
    Exeunt. Enter FLOORSWEEPER.

FLOORSWEEPER: Now there's going to be a wedding.
    Mightn't you have known.

Well, I'll get roast chicken.
And there'll be chicken for the cats,
Which have all come running back with their tails in the air
And for the dogs there'll be venison.
Feeding, feeding, feeding,
Sleeping, feeding and marrying—
Trampling the floors, scattering the crumbs,
Somebody has to sweep them.
And the girl's recovered.
Why, it's simply amazing!
Her ailment's turned into a husband.
Wonders will never cease.

Sean, the Fool, the Devil
and the Cats

Characters

FOOL

MOTHER

SEAN

FIRST VOICE

SECOND VOICE

THIRD VOICE

FOURTH VOICE

CAT (miaowing)

DEVIL

MR. POPPACOPOLIS

FIRST WORKER

SECOND WORKER

THIRD WORKER

MISS POPPACOPOLIS

Sean, the Fool, the Devil and the Cats

Music

FOOL: Once upon a time—not very long ago—I was a happy
man.

But that's another story.

Now I'm blind, I've no ears, I'm a quilt of scars.

Look at me. Now listen.

There was a boy called Sean.

Not me. Sean was himself.

I'm a fool. Sean was clever. Now listen.

Sean was leaving home.

MOTHER: You're leaving me alone. O Sean, who'll look after
me?

SEAN: The neighbours will look after you. Our savings will
look after you. Good-bye, Mother.

MOTHER: O Sean, where will you go?

Get a job in a bank, get a job on a farm,

Get a job in a canning factory, keep out of harm.

Get a job driving a lorry, if you want to see the world,

But don't go away, don't leave me.

SEAN: I'm going for a year.

MOTHER: You're a dreamer, Sean. You stay at home. The
world will eat you up.

SEAN: I'm going to try my luck. So wish me luck.

MOTHER: Don't go, Sean.

SEAN: I'm going.

MOTHER: Then may an angel go before you, an angel behind you,

An angel to the right of you, an angel to the left,

All lucky angels.

SEAN: Good-bye, Mother.

MOTHER: Write to me, write to me.

Music.

FOOL: Sean is on the road.

He walks at the roadside in the dust of the cars,

In the exhaust of the diesels,

The racket of the trucks. His head begins to ache.

SEAN: Where does the road go?

A road goes to a road.

Roads run into roads, fork into roads, circle and come back into roads.

Roads can never get away from roads.

Roads are a maze with no ending.

People who stick to the roads stick to the maze.

They all end up where they started.

Get off the road, Sean.

FOOL: Sean turns up a lane, over a hill,

Over a bridge, and he stops at a crossroads.

It is evening.

SEAN: The sun is setting. Where shall I sleep?

Four roads meet under my feet.

Which one shall I take?

FIRST VOICE [*very distant*]: This way, Sean. This way for happiness, Sean. We like you. We like you. This way for smiles and presents and kisses.

SECOND VOICE [*distant*]: This way, Sean, for thrills and adventures. This way for hair on end and the skin of your teeth and the luck of the devil. This way for the

82

seven deadly seas.

THIRD VOICE [*distant*—MOTHER'*s voice*]: Come home, Sean,
come home. Wait a year, go next summer, think about
it, remember your bed. Remember your old dog.
Remember my puddings.

FOURTH VOICE [*close and urgent*]: This way, Sean, for a future.
You're just the chap we need—the very man. Just what
we're wanting—this way, Sean. There's a fortune in it.
For you, Sean. A good sound job with a good sound
future.

SEAN: Down every road of the four—there's a tempting voice.
But what about that stile in the hedge? And the path
that goes over the field beyond into that dark wood?
That's a fifth way. How about that?

FIRST VOICE: No.

SECOND VOICE: No.

THIRD VOICE: Don't go that way, whatever you do.

FOURTH VOICE: Good-bye for ever, Sean, if you go that way.

SEAN: Why, what's wrong with it? It's only a path to a wood.

THIRD VOICE: No.

FOURTH VOICE: Don't go that way.

SEAN: Right, then I'll try it.

FOOL: Who's that? Halt. Give me a light.

SEAN: Did somebody speak? Or is it an escaped parrot?

FOOL: Down here in the ditch, fool. Under your feet.
Can't you see what's under your feet?

SEAN: A face in the ditch. Can't you get out? Do you want a
hand?

FOOL: Have you got a light?

SEAN: A match?

FOOL: A light—a lamp, a spot-light, something to see by—a
torch. Haven't you got anything? Yes—a match, if
you've got a match.

SEAN: I haven't got a match.

FOOL: Fool—wasting my time! How can I find my treasure
if I haven't got a light? It's black as a mole-hole down
here. I've got a pick, a mattock, a spade—I dig and I
dig—but what's the use? I can't see a thing. I need a
light.

SEAN: What is there to see?

FOOL: Treasure, fool, treasure. Here at the crossroads, a
huge treasure. Have you never heard about it?

SEAN: No, I haven't.

FOOL: An enormous treasure somewhere here at the cross-
roads. Everybody knows about it. And everybody's too
lazy to come and look for it. But I'm not too lazy. I'm
no fool. I'm digging and I'm going to dig. But I need a
light. Everybody who comes past here—I ask them for a
light. Nobody ever has one. What is the matter with the
world—everybody going round in the dark? Why doesn't
anybody have a light? How can I see the treasure in the
dark if I haven't got a light?

SEAN: You're the fool if you ask me. Are you going to dig the
whole crossroads up?

FOOL: There's a huge treasure here somewhere. It's in all the
old histories.

SEAN: Why, when you get it you'll be robbed, or you'll eat
yourself to death. Or you'll be too old to enjoy it. Or
you'll never get it at all. You'll just be an old worn-out
ditch-digger—penniless.

FOOL: I can see you're jealous. Look: I've already found a
shilling. I'm hot on the track. It's just that my luck's
bad, that's all. In fact, my luck's rotten. What have you
got in that bag?

SEAN: Sandwiches.

FOOL: I'll give you this shilling: you give me a sandwich.

SEAN: You give me your luck and the sandwich is yours. I
don't want your shilling.

FOOL: You can have my luck. I give you my luck.

SEAN: And you can have a sandwich. Now I'm going over the stile.

FOOL: What—into the wood?

SEAN: Why not—if the path leads that way.

FOOL: Good-bye, Fool. You'll never come out alive—haven't you heard? There's a devilish Laughter in that wood.

SEAN: A what?

FOOL: A devilish screaming Laughter. Nobody goes near that wood. You hear it at night.

SEAN: Probably a woodpecker having a nightmare.

FOOL: It's the devil, fool. Don't mock him.

SEAN: I'm not scared of the devil. Or his cat. I'm off.

FOOL: Fool! Fool!

SEAN: Good-bye.

FOOL: Fool!

Music.

FOOL: Who was that fool in the ditch?

He went on digging for his treasure.

While Sean crossed the field in the twilight.

SEAN: I'm not scared of a dark wood. [*He whistles.*]

The wood gets darker. The wood is as dark as the fool's hole in the ditch. [*He whistles more softly.*]

FOOL: He enters the wood. He stops whistling.

He daren't whistle. The wood is too dark. And silent.

SEAN: The roots of the trees are like bridges, tunnels, caves. The tree-trunks twist away up, into dark. Here inside the wood, it's already dark. The path winds in, I can just see it. An owl floats up to stare. Little feet rustle in the fallen leaves. Ought I to go back? What's that?

[*A cat miaows.*]

A cat!

[*Cat miaows, closer.*]

Puss, puss, puss, are you lost? I see two huge eyes in the

85

darkness. Are you a black cat? Do you live here? Cat,
you must be gigantic. Are you sure you're not a leopard
—with those eyes!
[*Cat miaows very close.*]
Is a black cat good luck or bad luck?
[*Miaow farther off.*]
The cat's going back, deeper into the wood.
[*Cat miaows, farther off, insistent.*]
Does it want me to follow? I'll follow it. A cat's a better
guide than none at all.
[*Cat miaows, farther off.*]
I'm coming, puss.
FOOL: Sean follows the cat.
He follows its miaows.
Sometimes he trips on a root, or snags his sleeve,
But he keeps going.
The cat comes to a clearing.
In the clearing—twilight again.
In the clearing—a house. Whose house?
Round, stone, a strange house.
The door is open. The cat goes in.
Sean follows the cat—into the strange house.
A strange one-roomed house.
A strange, vast fireplace, with a fire burning.
A strange, huge table—twice the size of a normal table.
A strange huge chair.
A strange huge bed.
A pan of stew, the size of a cauldron, bubbles on the fire.
The cat sits by the fire and it grins at Sean.
It's a cat the size of a big dog—
A strange huge cat.
SEAN: Who lives here, Cat?
Who's your master?
What a sumptuous smell, it makes me drool, the whiff of it.

Thieving or no thieving, I'll have some of that.
I'm hungry. And I'll eat.

FOOL: He eats. And he eats.

One bowlful isn't enough. Nor two. Nor three.

SEAN: What are you staring at, Cat?

Cat, your eyes are scary. They're too big.

Cat, you make me shiver.

Stop staring at me, Cat.

Here, have a bowl of stew.

FOOL: He gives the cat some stew. Look at that!!!!

He gives the cat some stew!!! He gives it some stew!!

Never forget that—give the cat some stew!

SEAN: Well, puss, we've cleared the lot up. What will your
master say to that? Who is your master? Why is every-
thing so big in this place? Look at this chair. Look at
that bed. Is he a giant? Look at those boots. Who could
wear such whiskery ugly boots—they look more like a
couple of muddy old sheep-dogs, flopped out, dead-beat.
Does your master wear sheep-dogs?

CAT: Miaow!

SEAN: What's that now, Cat? What is it?

[*Wild maniacal laugh in far distance—repeated coming rapidly
closer.*]

What—what—what's that? That's the Laughter. The
horrible Laughter. Is that your master, Cat? And is he
coming? I've eaten all the stew! I'd better hide. I can
hear the teeth in that laugh. Under the table. No.
Inside one of the boots? No. The chest, yes, into the
chest. Don't tell him, Cat, don't tell him where I've
hidden.

FOOL: Sean jumps into the chest. It's full of old clothes.
He burrows under. He lowers the lid. He lies hidden.
Breathing like a little snake.

Maniacal laugh erupts into the room. It is the laughing DEVIL, *as horrible as possible in all ways. He is panting and puffing among his laughs.*

DEVIL: What a day! What a glorious day it's been! What a wonderful day! Oh, I've had the time of my life. Any visitors, Cat? There's a strange smell. Let me tell you: just let me hear myself tell it all again. Listen. I've found a rich man's beautiful daughter. Why are rich men's daughters so beautiful? A strange fact, that is, very strange. And this is a rich rich rich man's beautiful daughter. Miss Poppacopolis!

And do you know what I've done? I've turned her into a—CAT! ·

(Wild shrieking laughs—subsides.)

It's years since I had a day like this. The chances are getting scarce, Cat. No good peppering people with the plague, sweeping whole cities away with the smallpox, levelling entire populations with paralysis—that's no good. Not any more. Doctors come with their needles and everybody's happy.

No. Now I strike for the mind. Not the body, the mind. Now I make people crazy. I don't make them sick any more, I make them crazy.

So now—instead of blasting this beautiful girl with elephantiasis—I just throw a mouse in her face and shout, "You're a cat!" And now she thinks she's a cat. She's gone cat-mad—she actually thinks that all she can do is miaow and lap milk and run after mice.

[Shrieks with uncontrollable laughter.]

What's that smell? Has somebody been here, Cat? Anyway, the girl will never be cured. Do you know what the cure is? Who could ever guess it? Do you know what it is? Three things. Three things.

Her father Mr. Poppacopolis owns ten factories.

A whole town of factories. What sort of factories?

They can fruit. What sort of fruit?
Raspberries, strawberries, blackberries and plums.
Well, the profits are huge. How huge? Take my word for it
The profits of the factories are huge.
But the workers get only tiny wages.
Mr. Poppacopolis keeps all the profits for himself. He's
    greedy.
That's why he keeps them: he's greedy.
And his workers get tiny wages.
So this is the first step in the cure:
Mr. Poppacopolis has to share all his profits equally
    among all his workers.
So if the factories make more profit, they all make more
    money.
If they make less, they all make less.
Doesn't that sound sensible? Does it sound like one of the
    devil's ideas?
The point is: he'll never do it.
So his daughter will never be cured.

The second step is this:
All his workers line up in a long line,
Each hold a stick or an umbrella,
And Mr. Poppacopolis
Has to run down the whole line of them,
And each one has to give him a whack.
There are thousands of workers—they'll kill him,
And he'll never do it. So his daughter will never be cured.

And the third and last step in the cure is this:
Somebody has to turn himself into a dog
And chase the rich man's daughter who thinks she's a cat
To the top of the fir tree in the middle of the rich man's
    garden.

At the top of that, hearing the barking
Of a dog that's no dog
The cat that's no cat
Will come to her senses and be cured.
But who'll ever think of doing that to cure her?
So she'll never be cured. Never. Never. O! O!
[*New shrieks of laughter—which suddenly stop.*]
Who's eaten my stew?
Cat, who's eaten my stew. Somebody's been here.
Somebody's eaten my stew. Stop grinning, Cat. Tell me.
Who? I'm going to die of rage. Who's eaten my stew?

FOOL: But he doesn't die. He rages and he rages. But after a
while he falls on to the strange huge bed—and he snores.
He snores, and as he snores he grinds his teeth.
As soon as Sean hears him snoring, he lifts the lid of the
chest.

SEAN: Good-bye, Cat.

FOOL: Out through the door. Away through the wood. Dark,
black as the bottom of a swamp is the wood. He
stumbles, he staggers, he drags himself up and he trips.

SEAN: Ouch!

FOOL: Thorns at his knees, knobbly snags at his temples.

SEAN: I'll have to get out of the wood before he wakes up.
Ouch!

FOOL: He keeps going. He gropes. He feels his way.

SEAN: Now I need the fool's luck—no matter how bad. Ouch!

FOOL: All night he toils in the tangles of the undergrowth,
the traps of the roots and the maze of the trunks. He is
melting away with sweat. His heart bangs in his head.
He is ready to give up. When he sees——

SEAN: Dawn! A golden light in the grid of the trees. That
must be the wood's edge and that must be dawn.

FOOL: He comes bursting out of the wood. And suddenly
there are no trees, no roots, no tangle—only a wide

smooth lawn. And he falls. He lies there gasping, in the dawn, in the dew. But somebody has seen him.

MR. POPPACOPOLIS: Hoy there! Who's that? What are you up to? Hey!

FOOL: A big barrel of a man, like a kelly. With a bald head. A furious face, waddling in blue pyjamas that are covered with pink elephants. Walking in the dew before breakfast.

MR. POPPACOPOLIS: This is a private garden. Trespassers prosecuted. Get out.

SEAN: I'm looking for Mr. Poppacopolis.

MR. POPPACOPOLIS: What do you want him for? At this hour of the morning.

SEAN: His daughter's ill.

MR. POPPACOPOLIS: That's no news. She's ill all right. She's crazier every minute. Every doctor leaves her crazier than ever. She'll never be cured. The doctors have given her up. She's a lost cause. She thinks she's a cat! A beautiful girl—and she thinks she's a cat.

SEAN: I can cure her! You see how I'm torn to tatters? I've run all night—as the crow flies, a beeline straight through the forest. I couldn't lose a minute, because I've got the cure.

MR. POPPACOPOLIS: What?

SEAN: I've got the cure.

MR. POPPACOPOLIS: Cure? How can you cure her?

SEAN: Where's Mr. Poppacopolis? Where is he?

MR. POPPACOPOLIS: Come back. I'm him. Me. Walking here on my lawns because I'm going off my head with worry. And you say you can cure her?

SEAN: Let me try. What can you lose? I dreamed it.

MR. POPPACOPOLIS: You dreamed it?

SEAN: More or less. What can you lose? An angel told me in a vision.

MR. POPPACOPOLIS: An angel?

SEAN: And I remember it all.

MR. POPPACOPOLIS: Quick. Get into action. If the angels are on our side—there's hope. What do we do?

SEAN: First, you gather all your workers together . . .
Fading.

FOOL: But what's that noise? What's the uproar? Dawn, 6 a.m. and there's a horde of people coming up the road. A cacophonous mob.
Roar of crowd—growing louder.

FIRST WORKER: Open the workshops.

SECOND WORKER: Open the doors.

THIRD WORKER: Let's get working. Let's get back to work.

ALL [*confusedly*]: Open the workshops. Open the workshops. Let's get back to work.

FIRST WORKER: Just because the Boss's daughter's gone crazy, he's closed down the factories. Can we stand for that? He's closed down the factories so our wages have stopped. Can we stand for that? Are the factories going to stay closed till she gets better? Can we stand for that? I say NO. NO and NO.

ALL: No, no, no. Open the workshops. Let's get back to work.

FIRST WORKER: His daughter might be mad for a lifetime. Can we wait?

ALL: Open the factories, open the factories.

FIRST WORKER: We know he's worrying himself to death over his daughter—but ought he to send all of us into deep mourning, too?

ALL: No, no, no, she's not our daughter. Open the workshops.

FIRST WORKER: Mr. Poppacopolis, come out. Get out of your bed and hear what we've got to say. If you don't open the factories we'll smash your house flat. What we can't smash, we'll burn. Then we'll smash the factories. Then